Trash to Treasure PineApple quilts

Gyleen X. Fitzgerald

FPI Publishing

Trash to Treasure

Pineapple quilts

Gyleen X. Fitzgerald

Trash to Treasure
Pineapple Quilts

Gyleen X. Fitzgerald

FPI Publishing

P.O. Box 247
Havre de Grace, MD 21078
www.ColourfulStitches.com

Book Design: Brian Boehm, iDesign Graphics

Cover Design: Brian Boehm, iDesign Graphics

Pattern Layout: Jean Ann Wright

Editor: Jean Ann Wright

Copy Editor: Barbara Polston

Photography: Conrad D. Johnson

ISBN: 978-0-9768215-4-0

LIBRARY OF CONGRESS CONTROL NUMBER: 2010926174

Dedication

To the online group of pineapple quiltmakers who created
the synergy that inspired this book.

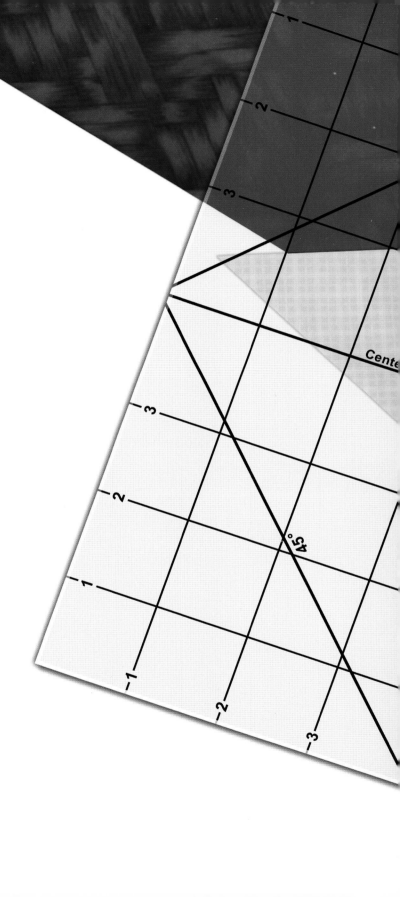

FOREWORD

From our initial meeting years ago, when Gyleen first expressed an interest in teaching at International Quilt Festival/Houston, to our current friendship, I have enjoyed a wonderful, colorful journey. During this time I have been treated to a view of the world through Gyleen's unique eyes. She encourages experimentation over perfection, experience over inactivity, and innovation over conformity. What a thrilling ride it has been! She has touched many hearts and minds with her enthusiastic approach to the world of quilting and we at the Quilts, Inc. offices have been excited to participate in the Pineapple parade!

After seeing her **Trash to Treasure Pineapple Challenge** on her *Haiku & Musings* e-newsletter, a few staff members began to excitedly cut their scraps into 1½ inch strips in preparation for some wonderful creations. Anticipation grew, more staff members joined in, and before you knew it we had nine projects going just among our staff! Lovingly referred to as the "Pineapple People," they have all worked with diligence and devotion — maybe even addiction — to see these various projects through to completion.

Gyleen's incredible initiative will result in an exhibit of **Trash to Treasure Pineapple Challenge** projects on display at the International Quilt Festival. Our staff is proud to be part of this wonderful showcase of the "fruits" of our labor. As is typical of her work

in general, Gyleen has managed to bring even non-quilters to the cutting table in search of their own Pineapple magic through this fun and exciting project.

I invite you to get out those scraps, ruler, and cutter, and get ready to become one of the "Pineapple People" as well!

Cutting salad strips
Using every scrap on hand
Produced joyful quilts.

What fun!

Judy Murrah
Vice President of Education and Administration
Quilts, Inc.

ii

Table of Contents

1

Introduction

Welcome to the **Trash to Treasure Pineapple Quilt** challenge. It's not a contest, but I am going to motivate and inspire you to get to the finish line.

This is how it all started . . . I finished up 20 or so antique quilts for my *Quilts: Unfinished Stories with New Endings* book and all but two were quilted on a longarm. Like many of you know, the quilt back must be made at least 4" on all sides larger than the quilt top to get loaded on a longarm quilting machine. The challenge is what in the world would you do with all that extra "good" fabric once you trimmed the quilt for the binding? Throwing it out was not an option. In my case, I kept thinking that in some future epiphany I would use it for . . . you fill in the blank.

Ha! I now have baskets full scraps (4" plus or minus in length), plus my normal bits of scraps left over from projects. They just kept multiplying as each new quilt was made.

Now fast forward to sometime later. Beth and I were at a quilt show and we were awe struck by an antique pineapple quilt on display. We commented that one day (famous last words) we would make one. Years passed and no pineapple quilt or block or cut strips appeared.

Today, armed with the **Pineapple Tool**©, we finally broke the inertia by grabbing our rotary cutters by the handle and getting a grip on all that trash! The plan is to spend a few months in front of the TV or a roaring fire and cut down all scraps from every nook and cranny into 1½" wide strips. All of them!

When that's done, the sewing will commence, block by block until there is at least one queen size quilt. I'm not even going to get concerned about coloring the quilt in the traditional way. Mine will be a full random mosaic; however, you can deviate from my plan at anytime as long as you promise to keep sewing. I've provided seven options, so, if you want a traditional layout, be my guest.

The whole point is to have fun as you sew with rapid abandon. Who knows how far the noodles, as I like to call them, will go? Let's just keep sewing noodles into pineapple blocks and then into a one-of-a-kind pineapple quilt until they're all gone. The plan is to live free of scrap clutter forever.

Take pause; those quilters of days gone by have nothing on us. We too can turn the most humble scraps into one stunning and absolutely beautiful artistic expression in fiber. I call it the **Trash to Treasure Pineapple Quilt.**

Go for it!

Tool of the
TRADE

Cut strips 1½".
Cut center square 2½" using ruler.

Round 1

Sew a strip to each side of the center square with right sides together using a scant ¼" seam allowance. Press each seam towards a strip as you sew it in place. From the wrong side of block, place the **Pineapple Tool**© so that the CUT edge of the center square is against diagonal lines and the center line of the **Pineapple Tool**© passes through cross points of stitching lines *(Diagram 1)*. Trim. Repeat on each side. Round 1 is the only round which uses the diagonal lines.

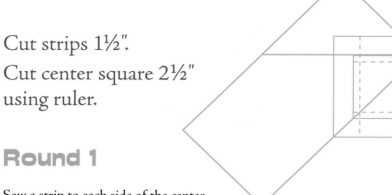

DIAGRAM 1

ROUND 1

Use a perfect ¼" seam or a skimpy ¼". Use up all that old bright colored thread. White, yellow, bright blue, or lime work well in the bobbin. You will need to "see" the bobbin thread so switch up if it's not enough contrast with your strips. The top thread can be any color.

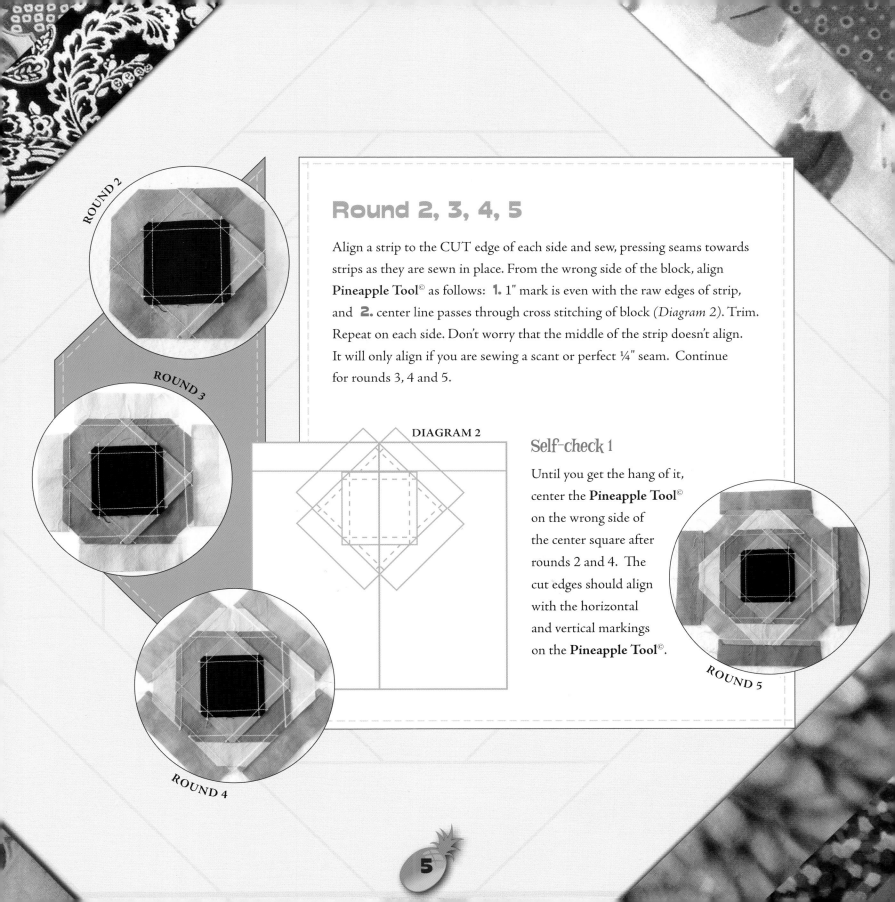

ROUND 2

ROUND 3

ROUND 4

Round 2, 3, 4, 5

Align a strip to the CUT edge of each side and sew, pressing seams towards strips as they are sewn in place. From the wrong side of the block, align **Pineapple Tool**© as follows: **1.** 1" mark is even with the raw edges of strip, and **2.** center line passes through cross stitching of block *(Diagram 2)*. Trim. Repeat on each side. Don't worry that the middle of the strip doesn't align. It will only align if you are sewing a scant or perfect ¼" seam. Continue for rounds 3, 4 and 5.

DIAGRAM 2

Self-check 1

Until you get the hang of it, center the **Pineapple Tool**© on the wrong side of the center square after rounds 2 and 4. The cut edges should align with the horizontal and vertical markings on the **Pineapple Tool**©.

ROUND 5

5

Round 6

Sew a strip to each side; press seams toward strips.

Round 7, 8

Using a slightly smaller strip, center strip from Round 6. Sew, then press seams towards strips. Repeat for Round 8. (*Diagram 3*).

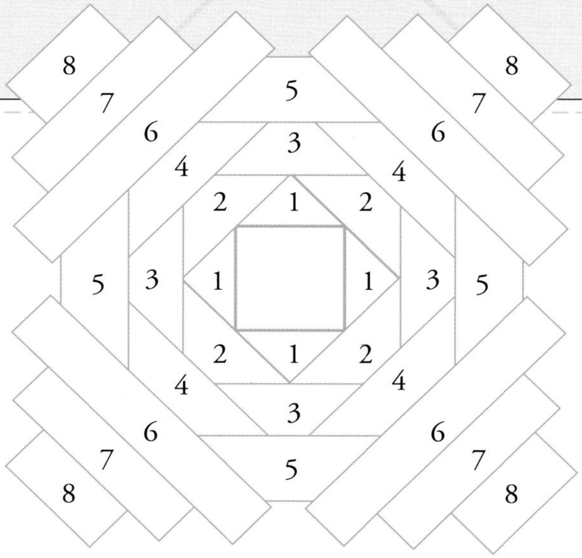

DIAGRAM 3

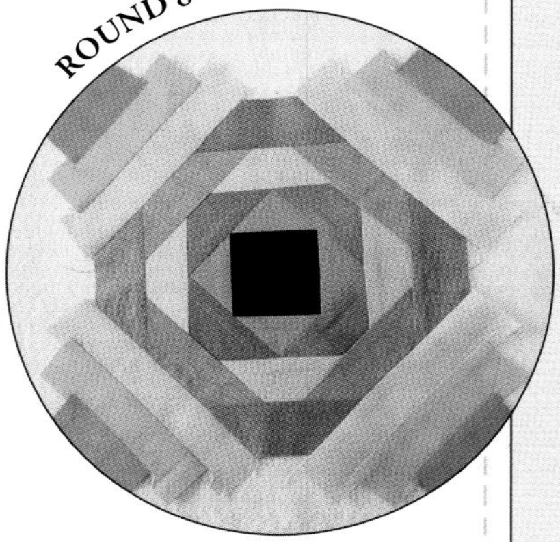

ROUND 8

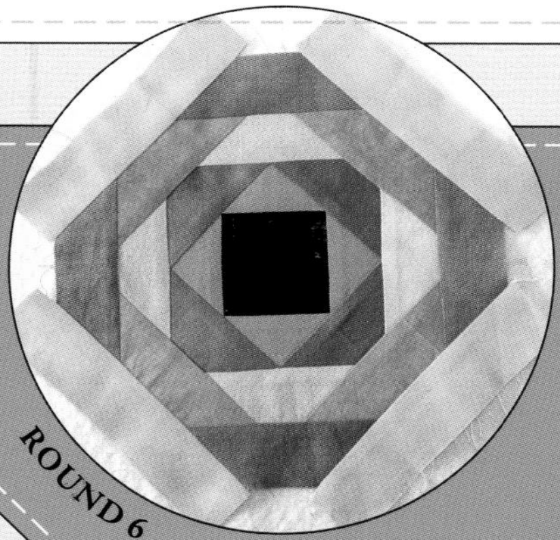

ROUND 6

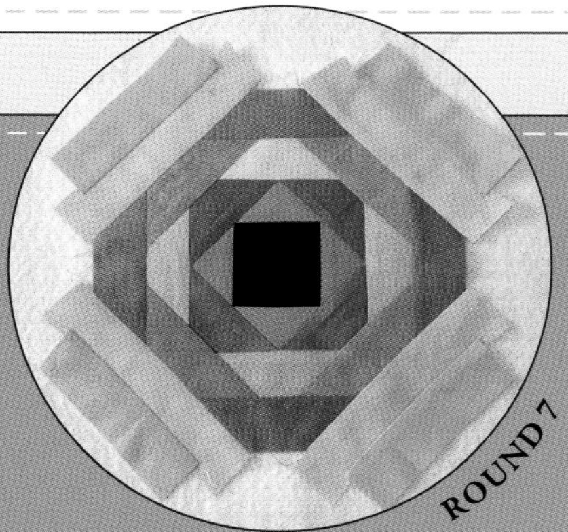

ROUND 7

I sewed the blocks together as I finished them, making two rows at a time. I needed instant gratification. I pinned (bias is on all sides) at each seam allowance when joining block to block but I didn't worry about matching seams! Matching seemed like a wasted effort since the blocks were so scrappy. I did make sure the seam intersections of the joined blocks were perfect.

When adding strips to the block, sew with the block on the bottom and the strip on the top with right sides together. Having 8" scissors is handy to shorten the strip. The final trimming of each round and squaring is done with the rotary cutter and **Pineapple Tool**©.

If you are making a block of divided lights and darks, sort them and put them in separate bags that can stand open for easy access. After awhile it's a pain to keep opening the bag.

To increase speed, I shuffled the strips in the bag and placed a gentle handful on my work surface. I used ONLY those strips to make the block. I pulled out any short pieces so I could use them up first. Some fabrics were used repeatedly in the block; just make sure the same fabrics don't touch each other. When the block was complete, I retained the less than 4" strips on my work surface, returned the remaining strips to the bag, and reshuffled them for the next block.

Squaring the block

Place the **Pineapple Tool**© on the wrong side of block. Align the 2½" center square with **Pineapple Tool**© marking *(Diagram 4)*. Trim block on all sides to 8½".

Self-check 2

Looking at the right side of your trimmed Pineapple block, each strip width should be 1" except round 5 which is 1¼" and round 8 was meant to be very small. Think of it as an embellishment.

Perfect!

DIAGRAM 4

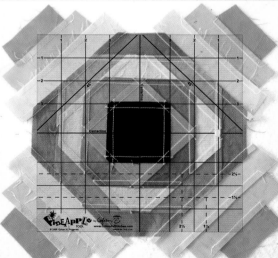

After awhile, you will be able to estimate the size strip you need for each round. Use the retained strips first. You don't want lots of little pieces at the bottom of your bag. The estimate for each strip length is:

Round 1: 2½"	**Round 5:** 5"
Round 2: 3½"	**Round 6:** 6"
Round 3: 4"	**Round 7:** 4"
Round 4: 5"	**Round 8:** 2"

The biggest thing to remember is to have fun; this is stressless, free-spirited sewing. If you're not happy, you're thinking too much. The more blocks you finish, the less concerned you will be about each fabric. Random will get easier. Blocks look better sewn together than when viewed separately. Just keep going no matter what.

Sliced
PineAPPLes
the Quilts

9

No matter how you slice it, it's still...
a Pineapple Quilt.

Following are seven quilts demonstrating my seven layout designs using scraps and a few yards of fabric from your stash.

1

Ends with Love

Totally random or mosaic. The center squares are the same color throughout all the blocks. No need to pick one fabric as a variety is nice as long as it's the same color and in the same tone. Borders match centers.

2

Obon Festival

Totally random or mosaic with scrappy 1" sashing. The center squares and cornerstones are the same color. The border coordinates with the center squares.

3

Harvesting Pineapples...
Out of Thin Air

Separate light strips from dark strips. The center squares are light and scrappy. Light strips are used on rounds 1, 3 & 5. Dark strips are used on rounds 2, 4, 6, 7 & 8. You can reverse the lights and darks.

4

Birds Fly Over the Rainbow

Scrappy and feature fabric. The center squares scrappy. Scraps used on rounds 2, 4, 6, 7 & 8. A feature fabric is used for rounds 1, 3 & 5.

5

Noodle Soup

Separate lights from darks and add scrappy sashing. The center squares and cornerstones are light and scrappy. Dark strips are used on rounds 1, 3 & 5. Light strips are used on rounds 2, 4, 6, 7 & 8. You can reverse the lights and darks.

6

Antique Rose

Monochromatic in a single expanded color palette. The color placement of strips are random or mosaic for all rounds.

7

Seaside Retreat

Separate light strips from dark strips. The centers are medium or dark. Rounds 5 & 6 are dark; and all other rounds light. This can work in the reverse; it depends on what you have in scraps.

Ends with Love

Armed with a huge bag full of 1½" strips, I sewed this quilt as free-spirited as possible. I used it all; novelty, juvenile, batik, calico and my "good stuff". I call this type of pineapple block a full mosaic. I was trying to think what attracts me to a mosaic and I think it's because it reminds me of a crazy quilt with some order in the piecing. I named this quilt "Ends with Love" because the final strip in the final block has the word "love" written on it. Appropriate, don't you think?

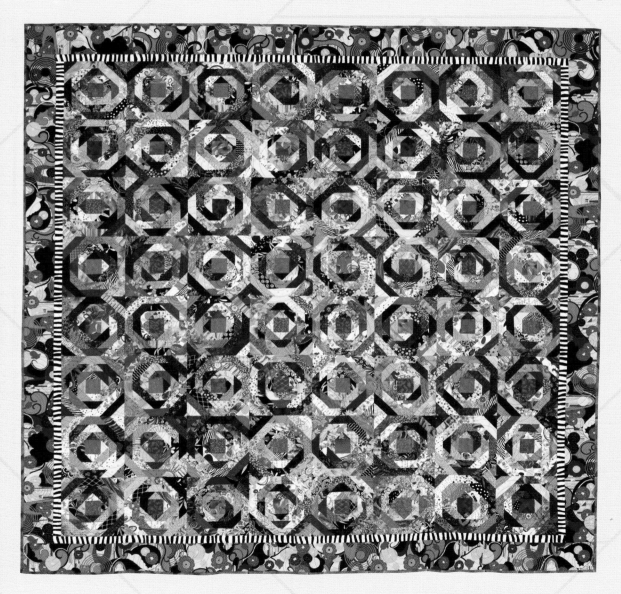

Quilt Size: 74" x 74"
Block Size: 8"
Block Count: 64
Quiltmaker: Gyleen X. Fitzgerald
Quilted by Beth Hanlon-Ridder

Supplies:

Assortment of scraps, lots of them, cut into 1½" strips. My guess is about 3 pounds worth.
(64) 2½" x 2½" squares, assorted fabric
1 yard for border 1
1½ yards for border 2
⅔ yard for binding

Special Tool:

Pineapple Tool© by Gyleen

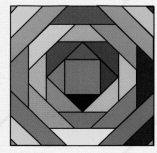

Pineapple Block

Instructions:

1. Follow the basic sewing instructions for making a pineapple block. Use 1½" strips of assorted dark, medium, and light printed fabric and semi-solids, randomly for all rounds.

2. Make (64) fully random pineapple blocks.

3. Sew (8) blocks together to form rows. I sewed my blocks together as I made them. Make (8) rows.

Row of 8 Pineappple Blocks

4. Sew row to row to complete the quilt top.

5. Using border 1 fabric, cut (8) 1½" x 40" strips. Sew the strips together end-to-end. Measure the quilt from top to bottom through the center of the quilt and cut (2) border strips equal to this measurement. Sew borders to both sides of the quilt. Press seams toward the border.

6. Measure the quilt from side to side through the center of the quilt and cut (2) border strips equal to this measurement. Sew borders to the top and bottom of the quilt. Press seams toward the border.

7. Using border 2 fabric, cut (8) 4½" x 40" strips. Sew the strips together end-to-end. Measure the quilt from top to bottom through the center of the quilt and cut (2) border strips equal to this measurement. Sew borders to both sides of the quilt. Press seams toward the border.

8. Measure the quilt from side to side through the center of the quilt and cut (2) border strips equal to this measurement. Sew borders to the top and bottom of the quilt. Press seams toward the border.

9. Layer backing, batting, and quilt top. I love circles and circular patterns and high density quilting. Beth quilted what looks like concentric circles in several sizes edge-to-edge using a medium red thread to match my center squares.

10. Using binding fabric, cut (8) 2½" x 40" strips. Sew strips together end-to-end. Fold strip in half lengthwise and press fold line. Align raw edges of binding to raw edges of the quilt top. Sew in place. Turn folded edge to the back of the quilt and sew in place.

11. Add label with your name and date. Add sleeve for hanging.

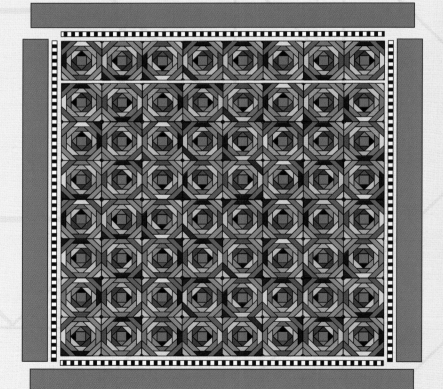

Quilt Assembly Diagram

Obon Festival

The Obon Festival is a celebration of heritage and an important family gathering time as people in Japan return to their hometowns. In preparation for the family gathering, houses are cleaned and family members offer a variety of vegetables and fruits to the spirits of ancestors. Beth tidied up her studio and found this extensive collection of Japanese prints. I love how the sashing flows fluidly through the quilt creating a graceful transition between blocks. Her quilt depicts the floating paper lanterns used during the festival.

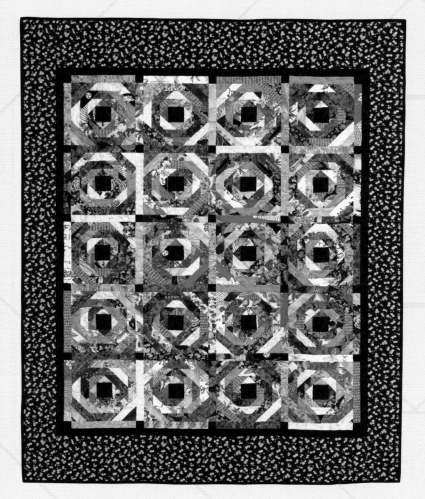

Quilt Size: 47" x 60"
Block Size: 8"
Block Count: 20
Quiltmaker: Beth Hanlon-Ridder
Quilted by Beth Hanlon-Ridder

Supplies:

Assortment of scraps, lots of them, cut into 1½" strips.
1½ yards for center squares, corner squares, border 1 and binding
1½ yards for border 2

Special Tool:

Pineapple Tool© by Gyleen

Instructions:

1. Follow the basic sewing instructions for making a pineapple block. Use 1½" strips of assorted dark, medium, and light printed fabric, randomly, for all rounds.

2. Using the 1½ yard, cut (20) 2½" x 2½" squares; (30) 1½" x 1½" squares. Make (20) fully random pineapple blocks.

Pineapple Block

3. Using an assortment of the pre-cut 1½" strips; cross cut (49) 1½" x 8½" segments for sashing. Alternate and sew (4) blocks between (5) sashing segments to form rows. Press seams toward the sashing. Repeat for (5) rows.

4. Alternate and sew (4) sashing segments between (5) corner-stones. Press seams toward the sashing. Make (6).

5. Sew the (5) assembled rows between (6) cornerstone-sashing assemblies. Press seams toward the cornerstone-sashing assembly. This completes the quilt's center.

6. Using border 1 fabric, cut (5) 1½" x 40" strips. Sew the strips together end-to-end. Measure the quilt from top to bottom through the center of the quilt and cut (2) border strips equal to this measurement. Sew borders to both sides of the quilt. Press seams toward the border.

7. Measure the quilt from side to side through the center of the quilt and cut (2) border strips equal to this measurement. Sew borders to the top and bottom of the quilt. Press seams toward the border.

8. Using border 2 fabric, cut (3) 4½" x 40" strips. Sew the strips together end-to-end. Measure the quilt from top to bottom through the center of the quilt and cut (2) border strips equal to this measurement. Sew borders to both sides of the quilt. Press seams toward the border.

9. Using border 2 fabric, cut (3) 6½" x 40" strips. Sew the strips together end-to-end. Measure the quilt from side to side through the center of the quilt and cut (2) border strips equal to this measurement. Sew borders to the top and bottom of the quilt. Press seams toward the border.

10. Layer backing, batting, and quilt top. Beth quilted a some-what formal key-like pattern edge-to-edge using a gentle tan thread.

11. Using binding fabric, cut (6) 2½" x 40" strips. Sew strips together end-to-end. Fold strip in half lengthwise and press fold line. Align raw edges of binding to raw edges of the quilt top. Sew in place. Turn folded edge to the back of the quilt and sew in place.

12. Add label with your name and date. Add sleeve for hanging.

Sashing Row

Block Row

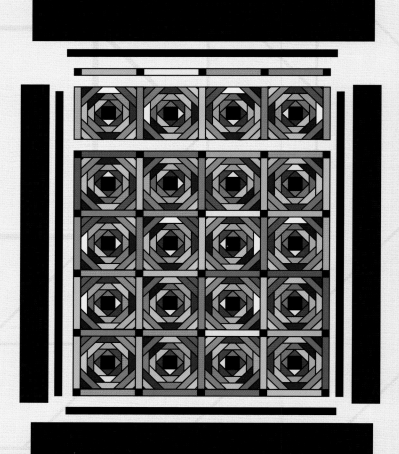

Quilt Assembly Diagram

Harvesting Pineapples...Out of Thin Air

In every crowd you get one who just see things differently. Mary Jo embraced this challenge with all her heart and soul, sewing until 2 A.M. on most nights. She produced this quilt from her scraps, some stash, and bits and pieces. She basically harvested her pineapple blocks out of thin air. As a longarm quilter, she is also plagued with having a 4" trim for every quilt loaded onto her machine. The key to duplicating Mary Jo's quilt is to sew the blocks together as you make them. Doing this will keep the secondary color pattern as the focal point.

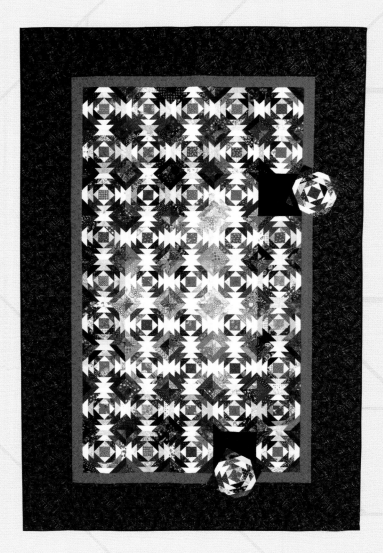

Quilt Size: 62" x 94"
Block Size: 8"
Block Count: 45
Quiltmaker: Mary Jo Yackley
Quilted by Mary Jo Yackley

Supplies:

Assortment of green, black, blue, and purple (four color groups) for feature fabric. You need approximately 2 pounds worth of strips. Assortment of lights, tone-on-tone, and pastel, large or small print. You will need approximately 1 pound worth of strips.
(45) 2½" x 2½" squares, assorted reds
(2) 8½" x 8½" squares, black
1¼ yards for border 1
2¾ yards for border 2
⅔ yards for binding

Special Tool:

Pineapple Tool© by Gyleen

Instructions:

1. Using the assorted green, black, blue, and purple, cut lots of 1½" strips; keep them sorted by color group.

2. Using the assorted lights, cut lots of 1½" strips.

3. Follow the basic sewing instructions for making a pineapple block. Use 1½" strips of assorted lights, randomly for rounds 1, 3 and 5 in all (45) blocks.

4. Now the tricky part, rounds 2, 4, 6, 7 and 8 form the diagonal piecing (on the corners) of the pineapple block. Using the green, black, blue, and purple, what you want to do is to keep the color group the same down that whole diagonal distance. You will end up with a different color on each corner and it will run to the red center square. See the sketch as this is harder to explain than it is to do.

5. I would highly recommend you make one block at a time and connect the blocks as you complete them so as not to get confused. There are 5 blocks per row and 9 rows complete the quilt top. In row 3, replace the 5th pineapple block with an 8½" x 8½" black square. In row 9, replace the 4th pineapple block with an 8½" x 8½" black square.

6. Using the border 1 fabric, cut (6) 2½" x 40" strips. Sew the strips together end-to-end. Measure the quilt from top to bottom through the center and cut (2) border strips equal to this measurement. Sew borders to both sides of the quilt. Press seams toward the border.

7. Measure the quilt from side to side through the center and cut (2) border strips equal to this measurement. Sew borders to the top and bottom of the quilt. Press seams toward the border.

8. Using the border 2 fabric, cut (8) 9½" x 40" strips and sew together end-to-end. Measure the quilt from top to bottom through through the center and cut (2) border strips equal to this measurement. Sew borders to both sides of the quilt. Press seams toward the border.

9. Measure the quilt from side to side through the center and cut (2) border strips equal to this measurement. Sew borders to the top and bottom of the quilt. Press seams toward the border.

10. Turn the ¼" seam allowance under for the two remaining pineapple blocks and appliqué them onto the completed quilt top. See photo.

11. Layer backing, batting, and quilt top. Mary Jo did some custom feather work in each block and concentric squares in the black squares.

12. Using background fabric, cut (8) 2½" x 40" strips. Sew strips together end-to-end. Fold strip in half lengthwise and press fold line. Align raw edges of binding to raw edges of the quilt top. Sew in place. Turn folded edge to the back of the quilt and sew in place.

13. Add label with your name and date. Add sleeve for hanging.

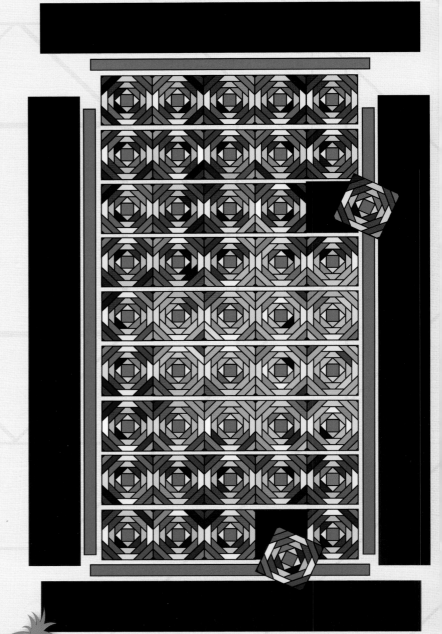

Birds Fly Over the Rainbow

Wow! Is it just me or does this quilt have impact? Barbara once told me her daughter's favorite color was rainbow and now I can see why. I love the echoing within each pineapple block, not really light to dark, but rather Barbara chose to build intensity as she added each round. And how did she do it?

Quilt Size: 42" x 42"
Block Size: 8"
Block Count: 16
Quiltmaker: Barbara Polston
Quilted by Beth Hanlon-Ridder

Supplies:

Assortment of red, orange, yellow, green, blue, and purple fabrics (six color groups)
2½ yards for background, borders and binding

Special Tool:

Pineapple Tool© by Gyleen

Instructions:

1. Plan to make (18) blocks so you will have options for your rainbow layout.

2. Using the assorted fabric cut several 1½" strips; keep them sorted by color group. Cut (3) 2½" squares from each of the six color groups for the center block for a total of (18) 2½" centers.

3. Using the background fabric, cut (18) 1½" x 40" strips.

4. The center 2½" square should be in the same color family as the 1½" strips for each pineapple block.

5. Follow the basic sewing instructions for making a pineapple block. Use 1½" strips of background fabric for rounds 1, 3 and 5 in all (18) blocks. Starting with the yellow group, use an assortment of yellow 1½" strips for rounds 2, 4, 6, 7 and 8. Make (3) pineapple blocks in each of the six color groups. Cut additional 1½" strips as needed.

6. Layout out blocks 4 x 4. Sew block to block, pinning the beginning and ending of edge to minimize stretching along the bias edge. Make (4) rows. Sew rows together to form the completed center area of the quilt top.

7. Cut background fabric into (4) 1½" x 40" strips for border 1. Measure the quilt from top to bottom through the center of the quilt and cut (2) border strips equal to this measurement. Sew borders to both sides of the quilt. Press seams toward the border.

8. Measure the quilt from side to side through the center of the quilt and cut (2) border strips equal to this measurement. Sew borders to the top and bottom of the quilt. Press seams toward the border.

9. Using the assorted fabric cut (56) 2½" x 4½" rectangles, these are your flying geese.

10. Using the background fabric cut (112) 2½" x 2½" squares. Fold each square, wrong sides together on the diagonal and press a crease at the fold.

11. To make the flying geese, place one square on top the rectangle aligning the two corners. Pin in position and sew on the crease line. Trim excess (to the outside of the rectangle), leaving a ¼" seam allowance. Press remaining triangle towards the seam allowance. See sketch.

12. Place another square on top of the rectangle; align square so that the crease begins on the same long edge as the first square. Pin in position and sew on crease line. Trim excess (to the outside of the rectangle), leaving a ¼" seam allowance. Press remaining triangle towards the seam allowance. See sketch.

13. Make (56) flying geese. Sew (13) flying geese together for the sides of the border 2; sew (15) flying geese together for the top and bottom of border 2. Make (2) of each.

14. Using background fabric, cut (2) 4½" x 40" strips. Using the (13) flying geese segments, sew 4½" x 40" strip to end with the flying geese point. Press seam. Make (2).

15. Measure the quilt from top to bottom through the center of the quilt and trim border 2 assembly strips equal to this measurement. Sew borders to both sides of the quilt. Press seams toward the border. See photo.

16. Using the remaining 4½" background strips and the (15) flying geese segments, sew together at the flying geese point. Press seam. Make (2).

17. Measure the quilt from side to side through the center of the quilt and trim border 2 assembly strips equal to this measurement. Sew borders to the top and bottom of the quilt. Press seams toward the border. See photo.

18. Layer backing, batting, and quilt top. Quilt an overall pattern to enhance the pineapple or rainbow design of the quilt.

19. Using background fabric, cut (5) 2½" x 40" strips. Sew strips together end-to-end. Fold strip in half lengthwise and press fold line. Align raw edges of binding to raw edges of the quilt top. Sew in place. Turn folded edge to the back of the quilt and sew in place.

20. Add label with your name and date. Add sleeve for hanging.

Flying Geese

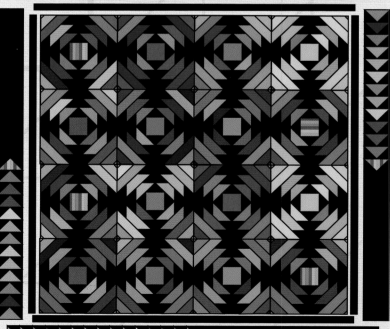

Quilt Assembly Diagram

Noodle Soup

Yum…it's one of my favorite comfort foods, noodle soup. Just looking at Gwen's quilt reminds me of a huge pot of my mom's soup; a soup without a recipe where you use whatever is in the refrigerator and each time you make it, it's different. Gwen was not fooling around; she was on a mission to clear her studio of clutter! She found all those hidden scraps and started cutting things down. All of it…producing noodles by the minute. Then, with determination, dipped into her stash for sashing and borders. Impressive what you can produce when you put your mind to it.

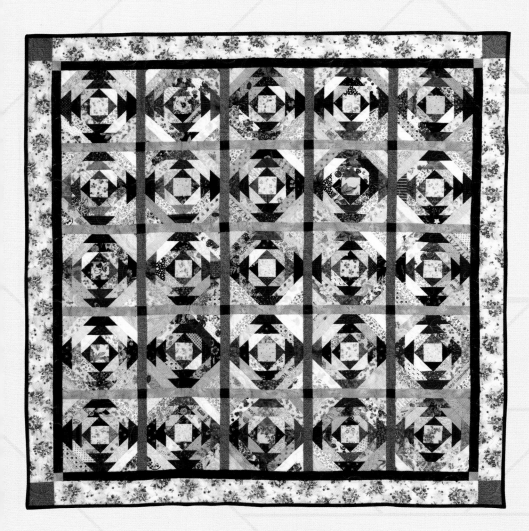

Quilt Size: 52" x 52"
Block Size: 8"
Block Count: 25
Quiltmaker: Gwen Ratliff
Quilted by Beth Hanlon-Ridder

Supplies:

Assortment of scraps, lots of them, cut into 1½" strips, separate by lights and darks.
(25) 2½" x 2½" squares, assorted yellow or cut from border 2 fabric
⅜ yard medium tone fabric for sashing
⅜ yard medium to light fabric for sashing
1 yard for border 1, cornerstones and binding
1 yard for border 2

Special Tool:

Pineapple Tool© by Gyleen

Instructions:

1. Follow the basic sewing instructions for making a pineapple block. Use 1½" strips of assorted darks/mediums, randomly, for rounds 1, 3 and 5 in all (25) blocks.

2. Use 1½" strips of assorted lights, randomly, for rounds 2, 4, 6, 7 and 8 in all (25) blocks.

3. Using the medium sashing fabric, cut (5) 1½" strips and cross cut into (20) 1½" x 8½" segments. Sew sashing between blocks to form rows. Press seams toward the sashing. Repeat for (5) rows.

4. Using light sashing fabric, cut (5) 1½" strips and cross cut into (20) 1½" x 8½" segments.

5. Using border 1 fabric, cut (5) 1½" x 40" strips. Cross cut (16) 1½" x 1½" squares for the cornerstones.

6. Sew (4) cornerstones between (5) light sashing segments. Press seams toward the sashing. Make (4).

7. Sew the sashing-cornerstones assembly between the rows. Press seams toward the sashing-cornerstones. This completes the quilt's center.

8. Using the remaining border 1 strips, sew the strips together end-to-end. Measure the quilt from top to bottom through the center of the quilt and cut (4) border strips equal to this measurement. Sew borders to both sides of the quilt. Press seams toward the border.

9. Using the remaining light sashing strips, cut (4) 1½" x 1½" squares for the cornerstones. Sew a cornerstone to each end of (2) remaining border 1 cut strips. Press seams toward the border. Sew border assembly to the top and bottom of the quilt. Press seams toward the border.

10. Using border 2 fabric, cut (5) 3½" x 40" strips. Sew the strips together end-to-end. Measure the quilt from top to bottom through the center of the quilt and cut (4) border strips equal to this measurement. Sew borders to both sides of the quilt. Press seams toward the border.

11. Using the medium sashing fabric, cut (4) 3½" x 3½" squares for the cornerstones. Sew a cornerstone to each end of (2) remaining border 2 cut strips. Press seams toward the border. Sew borders to the top and bottom of the quilt. Press seams toward the border.

12. Layer backing, batting and quilt top. Beth quilted a free-flowing, open leaf design using cream thread to complete the quilt.

13. Using binding fabric, cut (6) 2½" x 40" strips. Sew strips together end-to-end. Fold strip in half lengthwise and press fold line. Align raw edges of binding to raw edges of the quilt top. Sew in place. Turn folded edge to the back of the quilt and sew in place.

14. Add label with your name and date. Add sleeve for hanging.

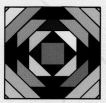

Pineapple Block

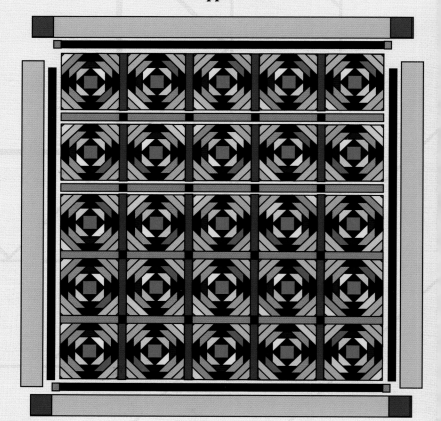

Quilt Assembly Diagram

Antique Rose

Oh, isn't this fun? Antique Rose is a monochromatic color wash of tan to blush to brown through grays of all things. It's the left-overs from a quilt back I made last year. Most of the fabric is from the Daiwabo Japanese fabric collection. I just never would have thought that what was fabric for a quilt back would someday become a quilt front. When I started the blocks it was my intention to omit the darker fabrics in the collection as I thought they were too dark. Well it just goes to show you, it's all relative since they worked perfectly with the medium colors. Needless to say, there isn't a bit of this fabric left in my house! Hooray!

Quilt Size: 52" x 52"
Block Size: 8"
Block Count: 25
Quiltmaker: Gyleen X. Fitzgerald
Quilted by Beth Hanlon-Ridder

Supplies:

Assortment of scraps in one extended color palette, cut into 1½" strips.
½ yard for border 1
1½ yards for border 2 and center squares
½ yard for binding

Special Tool:

Pineapple Tool© by Gyleen

Instructions:

1. Follow the basic sewing instructions for making a pineapple block. Use 1½" strips of assorted dark, medium, and light printed fabric and semi-solids, randomly, for all rounds. To get the color-washed affect use the dark strips sparingly in the light blocks and light strips sparingly in the dark blocks.

2. Using the center square fabric, cut (25) 2½" x 2½" squares.

3. Make (25) fully random pineapple blocks.

4. Arrange the blocks (5) across and (5) down in a pleasing color-washed blend. Sew (5) blocks together to form (5) rows. Sew the rows together to complete the quilt top. See photo.

5. Using border 1 fabric, cut (5) 1½" x 40" strips. Sew the strips together end-to-end. Measure the quilt from top to bottom through the center of the quilt and cut (2) border strips equal to this measurement. Sew the borders to both sides of the quilt. Press seams toward the borders.

6. Measure the quilt from side to side through the center of the quilt and cut (2) border strips equal to this measurement. Sew the borders to the top and bottom of the quilt. Press seams toward the borders.

7. Using border 2 fabric, cut (5) 5½" x 40" strips. Sew the strips together end-to-end. Measure the quilt from top to bottom through the center of the quilt and cut (2) border strips equal to this measurement. Sew the borders to both sides of the quilt. Press seams toward the border.

8. Measure the quilt from side to side through the center of the quilt and cut (2) border strips equal to this measurement. Sew the borders to the top and bottom of the quilt. Press seams toward the borders.

9. Layer backing, batting, and quilt top. Beth used a very dense, old-fashioned, rose and leaf pattern edge-to-edge with a tan/taupe thread. The pattern mimicked the toile border fabric.

10. Using binding fabric, cut (8) 2½" x 40" strips. Sew strips together end-to-end. Fold strip in half lengthwise and press fold line. Align raw edges of binding to raw edges of the quilt top. Sew in place. Turn folded edge to the back of the quilt and sew in place.

11. Add label with your name and date. Add sleeve for hanging.

Pineapple Block

Row of Pineapple Blocks

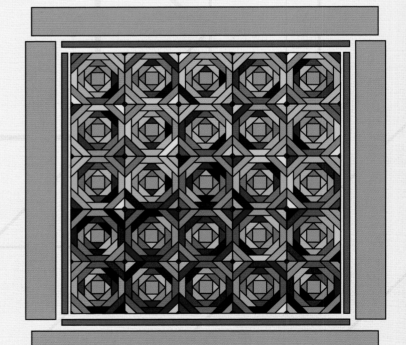

Quilt Assembly Diagram

Seaside Retreat

Jean Ann's quilt reminds me of marble floor in one of those luxury spas or is that just wishful thinking? My eyes seem to follow the dark chains surrounding the softly pieced pineapple blocks. Jean Ann auditioned several fabrics for the center square from light, which was nice but no spark, to dark, which was too dominant, then settled on this wonderful sea-teal, which keeps the eye moving from borders through the quilt to the block centers. Her choice of a brown, tan and teal color palette is very gentle and striking.

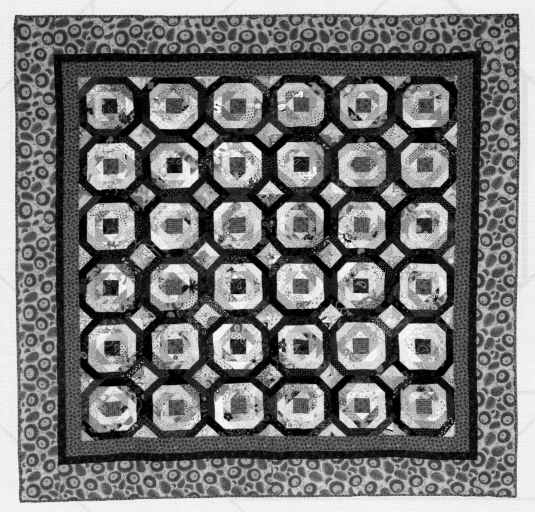

Quilt Size: 64" x 64"
Block Size: 8"
Block Count: 36
Quiltmaker: Jean Ann Wright
Quilted by Jean Ann Wright

Supplies:

Assortment of light scraps, lots of them, cut into 1½" strips
Assortment of dark scraps, cut into 1½" strips
⅔ yard for border 1 and center squares
½ yard dark for border 2
1½ yards for border 3
⅔ yard for binding

Special Tool:

Pineapple Tool© by Gyleen

Instructions:

1. Follow the basic sewing instructions for making a pineapple block. Use 1½" strips of assorted dark for rounds 5 and 6. Use 1½" strips of assorted light for rounds 1, 2, 3, 4, 7 and 8.

2. Using the center square fabric, cut (36) 2½" x 2½" squares. Make (36) pineapple blocks. See sketch.

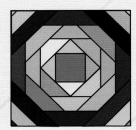

3. Arrange blocks (6) across and (6) down. Sew block to block to form the rows. Sew rows together to complete the quilt top. See photo.

4. Using border 1 fabric, cut (5) 2½" x 40" strips. Sew the strips together end-to-end. Measure the quilt from top to bottom through the center of the quilt and cut (2) border strips equal to this measurement. Sew borders to both sides of the quilt. Press seams toward the border.

5. Measure the quilt from side to side through the center of the quilt and cut (2) border strips equal to this measurement. Sew borders to the top and bottom of the quilt. Press seams toward the border.

6. Using border 2 fabric, cut (5) 1½" x 40" strips. Sew the strips together end-to-end. Measure the quilt from top to bottom through the center of the quilt and cut (2) border strips equal to this measurement. Sew borders to both sides of the quilt. Press seams toward the border.

7. Measure the quilt from side to side through the center of the quilt and cut (2) border strips equal to this measurement. Sew borders to the top and bottom of the quilt. Press seams toward the border.

8. Using border 3 fabric, cut (7) 5½" x 40" strips. Sew the strips together end-to-end. Measure the quilt from top to bottom through the center of the quilt and cut (2) border strips equal to this measurement. Sew borders to both sides of the quilt. Press seams toward the border.

9. Measure the quilt from side to side through the center of the quilt and cut (2) border strips equal to this measurement. Sew borders to the top and bottom of the quilt. Press seams toward the border.

10. Layer backing, batting, and quilt top. Jean Ann quilted a flowing meandering pattern through the blocks to emphasize the chain pattern of the dark strips.

11. Using binding fabric, cut (7) 2½" x 40" strips. Sew strips together end-to-end. Fold strip in half lengthwise and press fold line. Align raw edges of binding to raw edges of the quilt top. Sew in place. Turn folded edge to the back of the quilt and sew in place.

12. Add label with your name and date. Add sleeve for hanging.

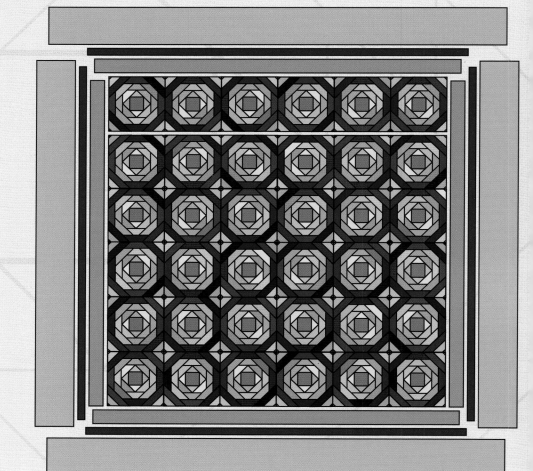

Quilt Assembly Diagram

Design Your Own

Overall Size: 74.00 by 74.00 inches

Design Your Own with Sashings

Overall Size: 72.00 by 72.00 inches

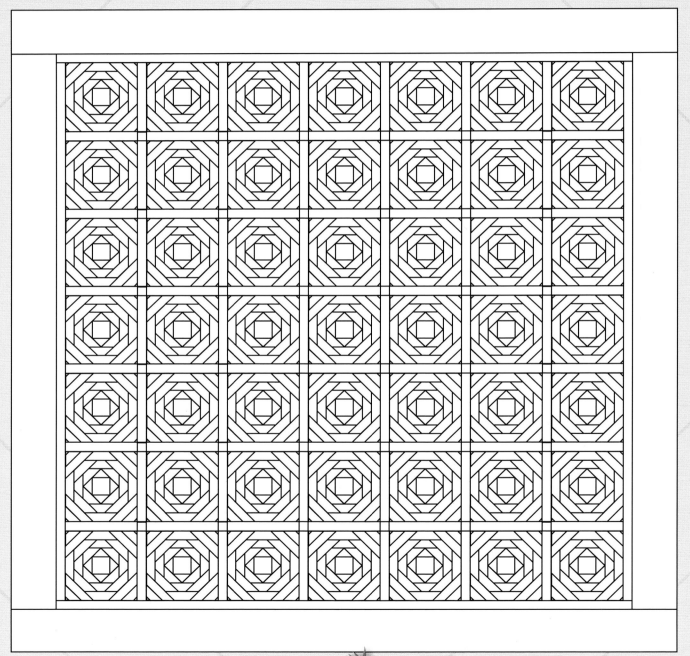

From the
Kitchen

One can't live by pineapples alone

... or can we?

Early Americans fell in love with the exotic qualities of pineapples while visiting their Caribbean neighbors. Back then, the trade route to get the fruit to America was full of drama. It was a heck of an achievement for a hostess to be able to produce a perfectly ripe pineapple for her honored guest. Oh, the things we do for company! It was a custom in New England to place a pineapple outside the entry door to signify a safe return. Nowadays, we literally put the pineapple up on a pedestal and make

it the centerpiece on everything from quilts to linen to furniture to tableware by carving, painting, or needlework. Today, it still says, "Welcome" and carries with it a smile.

As the quilters gathered to stitch their **Trash to Treasure Pineapple** blocks they continued the theme with mouthwatering hospitality. Here are some of their recipes...

Pineapple Angel Cake
from Glennis

1 box angel food cake mix
1 can of crushed pineapples, undrained
1 package of frozen strawberries, sliced
1 container of non-dairy topping

Mix cake mix and crushed pineapple until well blended. Spray 9x13 baking pan with cooking spray. Pour batter in pan and bake at 350° for 30 minutes or until toothpick inserted in middle comes out clean. Cool completely. Thaw 1 package of sliced, frozen strawberries and spread over the cake when cool then frost with a non-dairy topping and refrigerate. Serve.

Pineapple/Blueberry Scrap Cake
from Eleanor

1 tall can crushed pineapples with natural juice, undrained

3 cups fresh or frozen blueberries

¾ cup sugar

1 box of yellow cake mix

1 stick of butter, melted

1 cup of shredded coconut

1 cup of chopped pecans

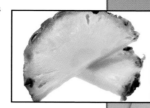

Preheat oven to 350° degrees and butter 9 x 13 baking dish. Pour can of pineapples into baking dish. Coat blueberries with sugar and pour on top of pineapple. Sprinkle dry cake mix on top of blueberries. Drizzle with melted butter over top of cake mix. Top with coconut and pecans. If you love cinnamon, as I do, you can sprinkle some on top before putting in oven. Bake 1 hour. Let cool thoroughly, if you can wait, then serve.

Pineapple Chutney
from Jean Ann

Crushed pineapples, drained from medium can (set juice aside)

½ cup orange marmalade

¼ cup red onion, diced fine

½ fresh red pepper diced very fine

1 tbsp fresh cilantro

1–2 pounds of sliced roast chicken

12–18 finger rolls

Brown onions in fry pan until almost caramelized. Add red pepper and cilantro and continue stirring until pepper is softened. Remove from pan and place into bowl. Add crushed pineapple and orange marmalade and stir together. Finished chutney should be a moist, pasty texture (add pineapple juice to moisten slightly if needed). Slice finger rolls (almost through) and add 1–2 slices of chicken, top with chutney.

Pineapple Chess Pie
from Beth

1 cup crushed pineapple, drained

2 cups sugar

¼ tsp salt

1 tbsp cornstarch

1 cup flaked coconut

4 eggs, lightly beaten

¼ cup butter, melted

1 tsp vanilla extract

1 (9 inch) pie shell, baked

Combine all of the ingredients. Pour into baked pie shell. Bake at 350° for 30–40 minutes. Cover crust with aluminum foil after 20 minutes, if getting too brown.

Enjoy!

Pineapple Cream Pie
from Judy

2 cups milk

1 cup sugar

3 tbsp flour

¼ tsp salt

3 slightly beaten egg yolks

1 tsp vanilla

1 small can crushed pineapple thoroughly drained

1 prepared pie crust, baked

Cook milk over moderate heat until warm. Add mixture of flour, salt, and sugar. Stir constantly. When mixture starts to thicken add egg yolks. I use a wire whisk to stir briskly. Stir constantly until mixture thickens and boils. Boil and stir for 2 minutes. Add vanilla. Stir in drained pineapple. Pour into baked pie shell.

Remember to add the meringue.

Pineapple Cream Pie Meringue
from Judy's Mom

3 egg whites, room temperature

¼ tsp cream of tarter

½ cup sugar

Beat egg whites on high with heavy mixer and blade. Add cream of tarter once you have started mixing. When egg whites are just starting to get thick slowly add sugar as whites are beating. Continue beating until soft peaks form. Stop beater when you think meringue is ready and lift with spatula. If peaks remain for a couple of seconds then it is ready. It's hard to over beat, but very easy to under beat the egg whites.

Put meringue on top of the pie filling with a spatula, lifting to form peaks. Bake at 350° for 10–15 minutes until lightly browned.

30

Pineapple Chunks
Bonus Block

Cutting

Cut strips 1½"
Cut (1) center square 2½" x 2½"
Cut (6) 3½" x 3½" squares, then cut on diagonal once for (12) triangles.

Round 1

Sew a strip to each side of the center square with right sides together using a scant ¼" seam allowance. Press each seam towards a strip as you sew it in place. From the wrong side of block, place the **Pineapple Tool**© so that the CUT edge of the center square is against diagonal lines and the center line of the **Pineapple Tool**© passes through cross points of stitching lines (*Diagram 1*). Trim. Repeat on each side.

Round 2

Center a triangle to the CUT edge of each side and sew, pressing seams towards triangle as they are sewn in place. From the wrong side of block align **Pineapple Tool**© as follows: **1.** 1" mark on the vertical and horizontal is even with raw edges of center square, and **2.** the triangle is in the corner of the tool (*Diagram 2*). Trim triangle. Repeat for each corner.

Round 3

Sew a strip to each side of the block. Press each seam toward strip as you sew it in place. From the wrong side of block, place the **Pineapple Tool**© so that the CUT edge of the triangle is against diagonal lines and the centerline of the **Pineapple Tool**© passes through cross points of stitching lines (*Diagram 1*). Trim. Repeat on each side.

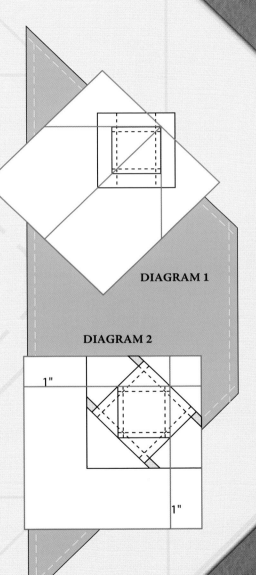

DIAGRAM 1

DIAGRAM 2

1"

1"

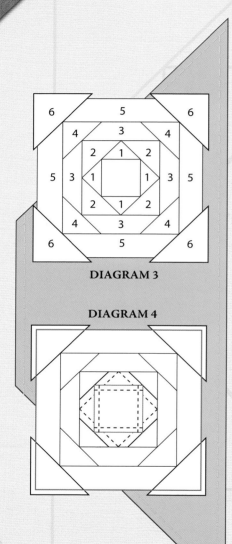

DIAGRAM 3

DIAGRAM 4

Round 4

Center a triangle to the CUT edge of each side and sew, pressing seams towards triangle as they are sewn in place. From the wrong side of block align **Pineapple Tool**© as follows: **1.** 1" mark on the vertical and horizontal is even with the raw edges of strip, and **2.** the triangle is in the corner of the tool *(Diagram 2)*. Trim triangle. Repeat for each corner.

TiP: Until you get the hang of it, center the **Pineapple Tool**© on the wrong side of the center square after rounds 2 and 4. The cut edges should align with the horizontal and vertical markings on the **Pineapple Tool**©.

Round 5

Sew a strip to each side of the block. Press each seam toward strip as you sew it in place. From the wrong side of block, place the **Pineapple Tool**© so that the CUT edge of the triangle is against diagonal lines and the center-line of the **Pineapple Tool**© passes through cross points of stitching lines *(Diagram 1)*. Trim. Repeat on each side.

Round 6

Center a triangle to the CUT edge of each side and sew, pressing seams toward triangle as they are sewn in place *(Diagram 3)*.

Place the **Pineapple Tool**© on the wrong side of block. Align the 2½" center square with **Pineapple Tool**© marking *(Diagram 4)*. Trim block on all sides to 8½".

Perfect!

Dojo

Dojo means "place of the way" and I interpret this as the way to enlightenment. The nine Japanese pre-printed batik characters: luck, success, friend, health, dream, love, happiness, peace and faith, are schools one must pass through on the way to enlightenment. This quilt appears to glow by the high contrast of black to the blend of reds, greens, and purples. The addition of sashing in a large-scale, high-density print and black cornerstones creates the secondary pattern.

Quilt Size: 33" x 33"
Block Size: 8"
Block Count: 9
Quilt maker: Gyleen X. Fitzgerald
Hand quilted by Gyleen X. Fitzgerald

Supplies:

(9) 4½" center squares*
Assortment of scraps in a dynamic narrow color palette, cut into 1½" strips
⅓ yard for sashing
⅔ yard for border 1, cornerstones and triangles
½ yard for border 2
⅓ yard for binding

*try using an appliqué, block exchange, a pieced block or fussy-cut a printed fabric.

Special Tool:

Pineapple Tool© by Gyleen

Instructions:

1. Follow the basic sewing instructions for making a pineapple chunks bonus block, eliminating rounds 1 and 2. Use 1½" strips of assorted dark and medium printed fabric randomly for all rounds.

2. Using the ⅔ yard, cut (36) 3½" x 3½" squares; cut each square on the diagonal for (72) triangles. Make (9) pineapple chunks bonus blocks.

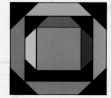

3. Using the sashing fabric, cut (3) 1½" x 40" strips; cross cut (12) 1½" x 8½" segments for sashing. Alternate and sew (2) sashing segments between (3) blocks to form rows. Press seams toward the sashing. Repeat for (3) rows.

4. Alternate and sew (2) cornerstones between (3) sashing segments. Press seams toward the sashing. Make (2).

5. Sew the (2) cornerstone-sashing assemblies between (3) assembled rows. Press seams toward the cornerstone-sashing assembly. This completes the quilt's center.

6. Using border 1 fabric, cut (3) 1½" x 40" strips. Sew the strips together end-to-end. Measure the quilt from top to bottom through the center of the quilt and cut (2) border strips equal to this measurement. Sew borders to both sides of the quilt. Press seams toward the border.

7. Measure the quilt from side to side through the center of the quilt and cut (2) border strips equal to this measurement. Sew borders to the top and bottom of the quilt. Press seams toward the border.

8. Using border 2 fabric, cut (4) 3" x 40" strips. Sew the strips together end-to-end. Measure the quilt from top to bottom through the center of the quilt and cut (2) border strips equal to this measurement. Sew borders to both sides of the quilt. Press seams toward the border.

9. Measure the quilt from side to side through the center of the quilt and cut (2) border strips equal to this measurement. Sew borders to the top and bottom of the quilt. Press seams toward the border.

10. Layer backing, batting, and quilt top. I hand quilted ½" down the center of each strip and ¼" on one side of the triangles using a dark watermelon thread. It's just enough to hold it together and avoid all the pineapple chunk seams. The border has an open cable using a stencil; however, I'm sure double wavy lines would have been fine since you can barely see the quilting.

11. Using binding fabric, cut (4) 2½" x 40" strips. Sew strips together end-to-end. Fold strip in half lengthwise and press fold line. Align raw edges of binding to raw edges of the quilt top. Sew in place. Turn folded edge to the back of the quilt and sew in place.

12. Add label with your name and date. Add sleeve for hanging.

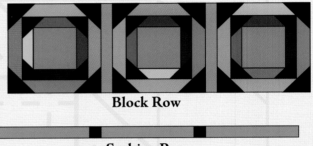

Block Row

Sashing Row

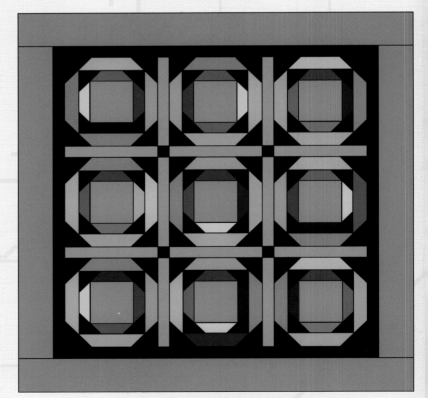

Quilt Assembly Diagram

PiNeapple Tidbits

Questions and Answers

Q: I assume it doesn't matter if I sew with the strip on top of the block or under the block.

A: Oh, yes it does! Sewing with the strip on the bottom makes the blocks grow out of control! Sew with the block closest to the feed dogs and the strip on top. The feed dogs make the bottom fabric move faster than the top fabric. (That's why they invented the walking foot). So, what is happening is you end up putting too much fabric down, which makes a wavy block. The block should ALWAYS go against the feed dogs so you can control the strip or you will need to pin the strip to the block, which I know everybody will hate doing.

Q: Do I need to pre-measure the strips before using them?

A: No, I hack them off as soon as I pass the needed length. When all four sides are on, I press, then trim using the **Pineapple Tool**© to keep the block square. I do keep all the short pieces close by so they can be used up in the next block. After awhile you can tell what will fit where.

Q: Hey, my strips look narrow after I trimmed. What happened?

A: I assumed when designing the ruler that the sewing might be less than perfect NOT THE CUTTING! It should still work even if the strip was not a perfect 1½". The trick is to align the next strip to the newly trimmed edges. As long as you have ⅛" remaining to hold on the next strip all will be just fine!

Q: How do you recommend quilting Trash to Treasure pineapple quilts?

A: This is such a personal preference question. Traditionally, pineapple quilts got an all over pattern or they were quilted within each strip (like log cabin quilts). In theory, you could go in the ditch but that would not be my first choice. Beth just stopped breathing at that thought. If I were (heaven forbid) to hand quilt, then I would do Baptist fans, hanging diamonds, diagonal lines, chevrons and the like; again an all over utility pattern. The other option for hand quilting would be concentric squares with quilting in the center of the strips.

I, for one, like edge-to-edge longarm quilting patterns. I've come to prefer high-density quilting that will hold a quilt together through repeated washings and loving. I see pineapple quilts as utility quilts which means full use and not going into the hope chest. Since I prefer a fun, pieced backing, I want the quilting to look fantastic on that side too! You may actually see the quilting better on the back, therefore, you might as well make a spectacular quilt back that will complement the front.

Q: Can I chain piece and make several blocks at the same time?

A: Sure; however, I sew one block at a time. Some do chain piece assembly style, which technically should be faster. I just have a rhythm for my way but you can develop your own. I also need instant gratification to motivate me to keep going.

Q: Can I plan where my strips are going to go ahead of time? I can't do random.

A: Yes, feel free to do anything you want. This is your quilt and will always be your creative energy. Go for it.

The more pineapple blocks you make, the easier they are to make. After awhile, you realize that any combination of fabric works. Personally, I'm addicted to total random. I don't want to think; I've got enough on my mind, like what movie to watch next! I so enjoy the WOW factor when I do the last trim and turn the block over. I find myself saying WOW every time.

Q: What do you do with all your quilts?

A: I have quilts all over my house…in every room and every spot possible for naps. I rotate them from one place to another often. The one on the foot of my bed changes every two weeks. I can't get enough of quilts. It's the one thing for sure to make me happy. More than dessert. But not more than my dogs!

So bring out your quilts, show them off, and make sure everyone remembers your love for them so when you die someone will care for them. They will love them because you loved them. What amazes me is my collection is nothing compared to other quilters that I've met on my journey.

CRushed Pineapples

Staying ahead of the clutter…

Fabric grows and grows in our studios overnight. I found that it doesn't matter how much square footage or how many shelves or storage boxes you have, we are getting paralyzed with over abundance. I do believe we have enough fabric right now for a life time. Gasp!

I can't stop shopping. I love fabric … all of it, new, old, and even ugly. I've tried several fabric management plans offered in books, magazines, and guilds over the years, but to no avail.

I've discovered if I use my stash I can replenish what I use. Quilting, every aspect of it, is my passion. I consider it something I can't live without. So I've come up an approach to manage the fabric remaining at the end of each project. Basically, I cut it down so that it's ready for my next scrap quilt. Here's what I do.

If the fabric is from selvage to selvage and has less than 6" remaining, cut it into strips starting with the largest size and picking what other sizes are possible: from 3" down to 1". Store them in labeled boxes.

If the fabric is from a fat quarter with less than 6" remaining, cut it into squares starting with the largest size and then what other sizes are possible: 4" down to 2". Store them in labeled boxes.

Gwen said that she uses photo storage boxes from her local craft store. They are beautiful and have a nice slot in the front to label what's in the box.

That should clean up your work surface. But what is in those boxes under the tables?

This is the "hard" stuff to cut because you jammed so many scraps in each box that now you need to iron it! I think ironing and odd shapes are the reason these scraps never get used. They are just perfect for a Trash to Treasure Pineapple Quilt. Cut everything down to 1½" strips. Smallest length needed is 2" and the longest is 5". No need to sort them, unless you must. No need to keep them flat either, unless you must. I keep mine in a large basket and a recycle bag, like the one from the Houston Quilt Show. It's important to use a big bag that will stay open. My "noodles" don't get crushed so they aren't wrinkled.

Cutting and collecting noodles never ends, but it can be neat and organized! ;-)

Acknowledgements

In quilting, we work together as a group to inspire, motivate and create. *Trash to Treasure Pineapple Quilts* is no exception.

First, I would like to thank Beth Hanlon-Ridder, who let me talk her into yet another huge project which appeared so simple in the beginning. Beth is the perfect journey companion, giving me her reassuring mother's confidence that everything is possible. She always had the answer to "what do you think?" as we travelled through the gauntlet of launching the **Pineapple Tool**©. She never pushed back or offered any "are you nuts" comments. Thank you, thank you, my dear friend.

When you really need something done they say to ask those already too busy for they know how to do more! Barbara Polston, Gwen Ratliff, Mary Jo Yackley, and Jean Ann Wright, creative and experienced quilters, who said, "Yes, I'll make a sample," without a pause. Those are not easy words to say based on their busy schedules, life to live, and unfinished quilts of their own needing completion. But each one, armed with a **Pineapple Tool**©, was committed to my vision that yes you can indeed make something from nothing. Thank you for being first to clear your clutter of scraps and to make five of the beautiful pineapple quilts showcased in this book.

Then came Quilts, Inc. where special exhibits are born. A huge, heart-felt thanks to Judy Murrah, who has believed in me from the beginning of my professional quilting journey. Judy was one of the first to sign up for my online group of pineapple quiltmakers. Her enthusiasm of "lets try something new — it will be fun", convinced several staff members of Quilts, Inc. to join the challenge. It was that energy, and several cut and sew days, that brought this project to the attention of Karey Bresenhan, Director of the International Quilt Festival, Inc.

Even now, I am humbled as I can't believe the number of quilters who embraced and inspired me throughout this journey. Your pineapple quilts are absolutely stunning. "Thank you" just doesn't seem enough, so how about a big hug one day soon?

PineApple TOOL by *Gyleen*

45°

Centerline

PineApple© TOOL by *Gyleen*

Cut from
Scraps or **Stash**

STRESS FREE & EASY TO USE

Put the **Fun**
Back in **Quilting**

MADE IN THE U.S.A.

www.ColourfulStitches.com

MADE IN THE U.S.A.

PineApple TOOL by *Gyleen*

© 2009, Gyleen X. Fitzgerald.

*Perfect accuracy…
without paper piecing!
Engineered for a
quilter by a quilter. One
tool for two designs.*

Price: $14.95

For More Information, visit: **www.ColourfulStitches.com**

Also available

The Dream
A Magical Journey in Colourful Stitches

Price: $29.95

ISBN: 978-0-9768215-1-9

Poetry & Patchwork

Price: $12.95

ISBN: 978-0-9768215-2-6

Quilts
Unfinished Stories with New Endings

Price: $34.95

ISBN: 978-0-9768215-0-2

LECTURES / WORKSHOPS

Gyleen is absolutely passionate about quilting and haiku poetry! Visit her on the web for patterns, note cards, and books, to schedule your group for her interactive lectures or workshops, or sign up for her free e-newsletter.

ORDERING INFORMATION

FPI Publishing books are available online or at your favorite bookstore.

For More Information, visit: **www.ColourfulStitches.com**

Gyleen X. Fitzgerald

Fitzgerald was born in Philadelphia, Pennsylvania, but grew up in Taiwan and Japan and now calls Maryland her home. She obtained a Bachelor of Science degree in Chemical Engineering at Drexel University.

Her quilts blend colour, pattern, and texture to provide a contemporary essence to traditional quilting. Her strength as a quilter is demonstrated by the infusion of engineering tools and techniques to simplify visually complex quilts. Her written works center around Haiku poetry, quilt patterns, magazine articles, and, of course, the crème de la crème, children's books. Her most recent book, *Quilts: Unfinished Stories with New Endings*, inspires quilters to transform orphan quilt tops and blocks into contemporary, finished quilts of today. As an artist she has achieved "Best of Show" recognition; as a writer, her journey is just beginning.

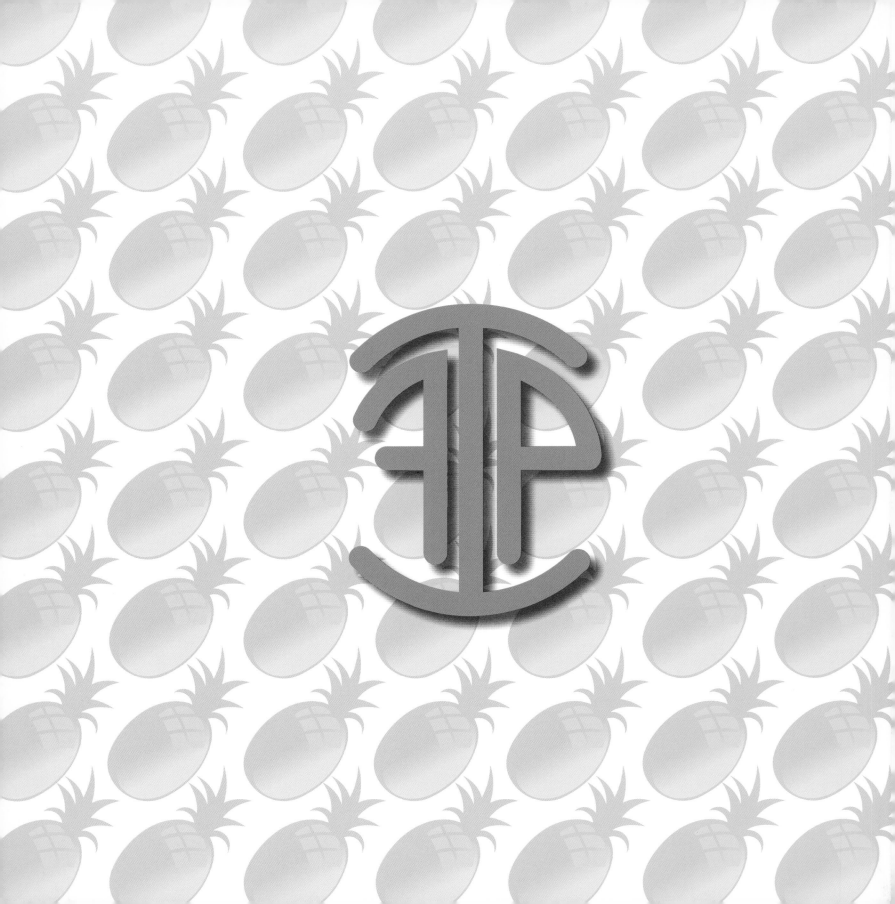